English Locomotion

参加して学ぶ総合英語

JACET　教材開発研究会　編著

音声ファイルのダウンロード/ストリーミング

CD マーク表示がある箇所は、音声を弊社 HP より無料でダウンロード/ストリーミングすることができます。トップページのバナーをクリックし、書籍検索してください。書籍詳細ページに音声ダウンロードアイコンがございますのでそちらから自習用音声としてご活用ください。

https://www.seibido.co.jp

English Locomotion

Copyright © 2015 by Mitsuko Yukishige, Hiroyo Nakagawa, Miwa Akao,
Sari Nishigaki, Yukiko Okamoto, Tomoko Onabe,
Kazumasa Ouchi, Ai Chida, Carl Nommensen

All rights reserved for Japan.
No part of this book may be reproduced in any form
without permission from Seibido Co., Ltd.

はじめに

　英語が特に得意ではなくても、皆さんはコミュニケーションを図るための英語力くらいは身につけたいと思っているのではないでしょうか。でも、もし思うように英語力が伸びないとしたら、原因の一つはその基礎となる文法力にあるのかもしません。従来、英文の構造や規則を学ぶ学習は、難しそうな文法用語を「憶える」ことが多い一方で、英語そのものを「使う」機会が少ない傾向にありました。そのため英文法を復習すること自体がおっくうだったり、退屈に感じたりした人もいるでしょう。でも、楽しいことをするのは誰でも大好きなはずです。

　English Locomotion の特長は、これまで忘れられがちであった「学習者が楽しみながら基礎語学力を発展させる」ことに留意した点にあります。文法用語は必要最低限にとどめられ、楽しみながら無理なく英文法の概念を習得できるように工夫されています。学ぶというよりは遊んでいるような感覚で自然に復習できるうえ、ただ構造や規則を確認するだけでなく、自分の意見を英語で発信できるレベルの運用力の習得を目指しています。「楽しく」学んだ英語を「使える」総合英語教材なのです。

　English Locomotion は、その名の通り、皆さんが英語の目標に向かって進むお手伝いをします。文字よりはイラストを多用した Warm up は、視覚的な導入による直観的な理解を助けます。また各章のトピックは、大学生活の中から特に楽しい状況のみを厳選し、身近でシチュエーショナルな場面が設定されています。「次はどんな場面かな？」と RPG（Role-Playing Game）型のゲームのような感覚でアクティビティに「参加」しながら、各自の個性を活かして興味のもてる分野で「使える」英語力を習得していきます。各章の Assignment は皆さんがその発信力を確認するための場となるでしょう。本書を通して、皆さんが楽しく英語に取り組み、使える英語力を向上させて下さることを期待しています。

なお、***English Locomotion*** は JACET 関西支部教材開発研究会第 12 次プロジェクトの開発教材です。言語能力だけでなく様々な知能に働きかけることによって、英語に苦手意識を持つ学習者にも楽しく無理なく英語に向きあっていただけるように配慮された教材です。本書がすべての学習者の英語力向上の一助となることを願ってやみません。本書の出版に際しては成美堂の菅野様に大変お世話になりました。この場をお借りして心よりお礼を申し上げます。

著者一同

CONTENTS

- **Unit 1** はじめまして！（文型） ... 1
- **Unit 2** レシピを見よう（自動詞と他動詞） ... 7
- **Unit 3** いつも何しているの？（現在形と頻度） ... 13
- **Unit 4** 何を持って行きますか？（名詞と代名詞） ... 19
- **Unit 5** あなたの理想の部屋は？（前置詞） ... 25
- **Unit 6** 目指そう！ 健康生活（助動詞） ... 31
- **Unit 7** 旅に出よう（不定詞と動名詞） ... 37
- **Unit 8** パーティーを開こう！（現在分詞） ... 43
- **Unit 9** 割れた窓？（過去分詞） ... 49
- **Unit 10** スポーツをしよう（現在完了形） ... 55
- **Unit 11** フリマでお買い物（形容詞と比較） ... 61
- **Unit 12** レポートの提出（関係代名詞） ... 67
- **Unit 13** どこに住んでいるの？（「それは」と訳さない It） ... 73
- **Unit 14** 宝くじが当たったらなあ（仮定法） ... 79
- **Unit 15** Review Test ... 85
- 人称代名詞一覧 ... 90

はじめまして！

あなたは留学生のパーティーに出席することになりました。1人ずつ、1分間の自己紹介をしますが、どんなことを話しますか。

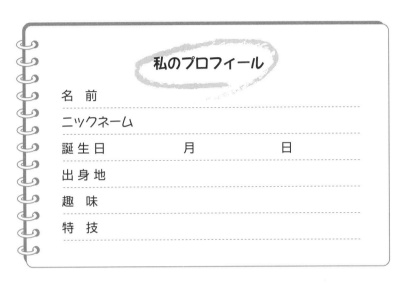

Warm-up （ペアワーク）

1. 上のプロフィールにあなたの情報を日本語で書き入れましょう。

2. 1. で書き入れたプロフィールを基に、下の表を完成させましょう。そして、ペアになって英語で自分のことを紹介しましょう。相手の友達の情報も、書き入れましょう。

	My Profile	My Friend's Profile
名　前	I am _____ .	He/She is _____ .
ニックネーム	Please call me _____ .	People call him/her _____ .
誕生日	I was born on _____ .	He/She was born on _____ .
出身地	I am from _____ .	He/She is from _____ .
趣　味	I like _____ .	He/She likes _____ .
特　技	I am good at _____ .	He/She is good at _____ .

Reading

 Tom と Homare の会話を読んで問いに答えましょう。 CD 02

At a welcome party for exchange students

Tom: Hi, nice to meet you. I'm Tom. (1)I'm a first-year student here at Star University. My major is economics.

Homare: Nice to meet you, too. I'm Homare. (2)My friends call me Homa. I'm from Japan. I'm a third-year student at Iroha University. My major is sports science.

Tom: I see, Homa. What does your name mean?

Homare: (3)Homare means "honor" in Japanese.

Tom: What a wonderful name! By the way, do you have a hobby?

Homare: I really like playing soccer.

Tom: Really? Me, too! Actually, I want to make friends with soccer fans. (4)I'll tell you my email address. If it's OK with you, could you email me later?

Notes exchange students ▶ 交換留学生　　honor ▶ 栄誉
by the way ▶ ところで　　want to *do* ▶ 〜したい

1. Tom と Homare について、下の表に英語でまとめましょう。

	Tom	Homare
大学名		
学　年		
専　攻		
趣　味		

2. 下線部 (1) 〜 (4) の文を分解しましょう。

	誰・何が／は	〜する／〜である	誰・何を／に	どんなだ	その他
(1)	I	'm (am)			here at Star University
(2)	My friends			Homa	
(3)	Homare				in Japanese
(4)	I	'll (will) tell	you/		

英語の語順

● 基本の形

The sun rises. 陽が昇る。

この基本の形（S + V）に、以下のような要素が付け加えられます。

● 基本の形 ＋ 補語（どんなだ）（C）

I am Kenji. 私はケンジだ。

● 基本の形 ＋ 目的語（誰・何を／に）（O）

I study economics. 私は経済学を勉強する。

● 基本の形 ＋ 目的語1（誰に）（O1） ＋ 目的語2（何を）（O2）

I give my dog some food. 私は犬に餌を与える。

● 基本の形 ＋ 目的語（誰／何を）（O） ＋ 補語（どんなだ）（C）

My parents call me Sachi. 両親は私をサチと呼ぶ。

Listening

1. ある男性と女性がパーティーで出会いました。音声を聴いて、下の情報を日本語で書きましょう。

(1) 名　前＿＿＿＿＿＿＿＿＿＿＿＿＿＿＿　　＿＿＿＿＿＿＿＿＿＿＿＿＿＿＿
(2) 出身地＿＿＿＿＿＿＿＿＿＿＿＿＿＿＿　　＿＿＿＿＿＿＿＿＿＿＿＿＿＿＿
(3) 職　業＿＿＿＿＿＿＿＿＿＿＿＿＿＿＿　　＿＿＿＿＿＿＿＿＿＿＿＿＿＿＿
(4) その他＿＿＿＿＿＿＿＿＿＿＿＿＿＿＿　　＿＿＿＿＿＿＿＿＿＿＿＿＿＿＿

2. もう一度会話を聴きましょう。男性と女性がそれぞれ自分の仕事について話している部分を聴き取り、下線部に単語を書きましょう。そして、どんなことを言っているか考えましょう。

Writing & Speaking

ある女優がハリウッドに進出することになりました。彼女のマネージャーになったつもりで、下の情報を基に、彼女の紹介をしましょう。（**Warm-up** の表現を参考にしましょう。）

浅田 さなえ
1997年 2月10日生まれ
- 出身地　　　　北海道
- ニックネーム　　サニー（Sanie）
- 好きな食べ物　　ハンバーガー
- 好きな花　　　　バラ
- 特　技　　　　ピアノ、スキー、スケート
- 趣　味　　　　読書、旅行

Her name is _____.
She _____.
She _____.
She _____.
She _____.
Her _____.

Assignment （ペアワーク）

1. 日本語に合うように、英語を並べ替えましょう。

(1) 僕は　大阪に住んでいます。
　　(live, Osaka, I, in) _____.

(2) 僕は　元気です。
　　(fine, am, I) _____.

(3) 私は　毎朝　ブログを　更新しています。
　　(I, update, every morning, my blog)＿＿＿＿＿＿＿＿＿＿＿＿．
(4) 私は　彼に　日本語を　教えています。
　　(teach, him, I, Japanese)＿＿＿＿＿＿＿＿＿＿＿＿．
(5) 私の友達は　私のことを　ミミと　呼びます。
　　(call, my friends, Mimi, me)＿＿＿＿＿＿＿＿＿＿＿＿．

2. 1. の (1) ～ (5) が答えになるような疑問文はどれですか。下からそれぞれ選び、記号を表に書き入れましょう。答えを確認した後、ペアで質疑応答練習をしましょう。

質問文					
答え	(1)	(2)	(3)	(4)	(5)

a. What do you teach Sam?　　b. What do your friends call you?
c. Where do you live?　　　　d. When do you update your blog?
e. How are you?

Let's Review! （文型のまとめ）

英語では、「主語（S）と動詞（V）」が基本の形です。

S + V	I study for an exam.　試験のために勉強します。
S + V + C S=C	I am a student.　私は学生です。 'I' = 'a student'
S + V + O	I keep a diary every day. 私は毎日日記をつけています。
S + V + O1 + O2	I teach you English. 私はあなたに英語を教えます。
S + V + O + C O=C	We call the cat Tama.　'the cat' = 'Tama' 私達はその猫をタマと呼びます。

Vocabulary　下の単語の意味が確認できたら、チェックを入れましょう。

☐ actually　☐ address　☐ by the way　☐ economics
☐ email　☐ hobby　☐ major　☐ science

Unit 2 レシピを見よう

留学生にあなたが料理を教えることになりました。どのような英語で説明できるでしょうか。

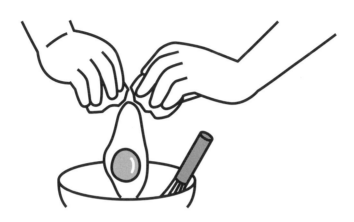

Warm-up

動詞を使って動作の指示をしましょう。（　）に下から選んだ動詞を書き入れ、文に合うイラストを選び、その記号を [　] に書き入れましょう。

(1) Please (　　　) in and (　　　) down.　　　　　　　　　　　[　　]
(2) Let's (　　　) these vegetables. Excellent!　　　　　　　　　[　　]
(3) Now (　　　) some salt and pepper, please. Very good!　　[　　]
(4) Let's (　　　). Beautiful!　　　　　　　　　　　　　　　　　　[　　]
(5) Don't (　　　) up, please. Lunch is not over yet.　　　　　　[　　]

[stand, sit, come, add, cut, serve]

　a　　　　　　b　　　　　　c　　　　　d　　　　　　e

Reading

次のレシピを読んで答えましょう。

これは何のレシピ？

A. (　　　　　　　　)
1. Put the milk and sugar in the electric blender.
2. Add your choice of fruit.
3. Blend until smooth.
4. Pour the shake into the glasses.
5. Serve immediately.

B. (　　　　　　　　)
1. Put the banana in a bowl and mash with a fork.
2. Add the milk and eggs.
3. Mix the banana, flour, sugar, and salt.
4. Cook, and then serve with maple syrup.

C. (　　　　　　　　)
1. Combine the eggs, water, salt and pepper.
2. Add some cream cheese.
3. Put the butter in the frying pan, and cook the egg mixture.
4. Serve immediately.

Notes
electric blender ▶ ミキサー　until smooth ▶ 滑らかになるまで
pour ▶ 注ぐ　serve ▶ 料理を出す
immediately ▶ すぐに　mash ▶ つぶす　flour ▶ 小麦粉
combine ▶ 混ぜる　mixture ▶ 混合物

レシピの出来上がりは何でしょう。料理名を下から選び、A〜Cの（　）に書き入れましょう。

Cheese omelet　　　*Fruit shake*　　　*Banana pancakes*

命令文

（You）動詞の原形〜
命令文とは目の前の相手に指示を出す機能があり、主語は省略されます。

● **自動詞の命令文**　　動詞は省略された主語（You）の動作を表しています。

Stop.　　　　　　止まれ。
Don't <u>run</u>.　　　　走ってはいけません。
Please <u>dance</u>.　　踊ってください。

● **他動詞の命令文**　　主語（You）の動作が 目的語 に働きかけています。

Fry the onion and pepper.　　タマネギとピーマンを 炒めなさい。
Don't <u>open</u> your textbook.　　教科書を 開いてはいけません。
Please <u>tell</u> your mother.　　お母さんに 言ってください。

Listening & Speaking （ペアワーク） 05

1. 料理の作り方の音声を聴いて、材料（名詞）と調理法（動詞）をメモしましょう。
   (1) 材料：
       調理法：
       Note：buns ロールパン
   (2) 材料：
       調理法：

2. ペアで何のレシピだったのかを話し合い、英語で答えましょう。
   (1) 料理名（　　　　　　　　）
   (2) 料理名（　　　　　　　　）

Writing

Warm-up を参考に、サラダのレシピを書きましょう。まず〔　〕に英語で材料を書き入れ、次に（　）に英語で調理の仕方を書き入れましょう。

レシピ名　　シェフ・サラダ
必要な材料〔　　　　　／　　　　　／　　　　　／　　　　　〕
調理の仕方〔add, chop, combine, cook, mix, serve, wash〕など

(1) (　　　　) the vegetables　　　(2) (　　　　) them into small pieces.

(3) (　　) some salad dressing, and (　　) well.

(4) (　　) immediately.

📁 Assignment

あなたは、ホストファミリーとしてオーストラリア人の中学生を家に迎えることになりました。家のルールをメモ書きで渡す必要があります。〔　〕内から語句を選んで英語で書いてみましょう。

〔take off, be quiet, make much noise, come home〕

(例) Please (be quiet) in the hallway.

(1) Please (　　　　　　) by 6 o'clock.

(2) Please (　　　　　　) your shoes in the house.

(3) Please don't (　　　　　　) after 10 o'clock.

📖 Let's Review! （命令文と自動詞・他動詞のまとめ）

- **命令文**　　　動詞の原形（主語がない）

  命令文の否定形　　Don't ＋動詞の原形

  Don't [run] !　走るな

  ていねいな命令　　Please ＋動詞の原形

  Please [go] .　行ってください

- **自動詞**（目的語が必要ない動詞）

  主語の動作や状態を表すだけなので、目的語は不要。

  Let's [sing] .　歌いましょう

  (e.g. dance, sing, walk, run)

- **他動詞**（目的語が必要な動詞）

  主語の動作が関わるモノや人が目的語として必要。

  [Add] some salt.　塩をいくらか加えなさい

  (e.g. chop 〜, add 〜, bake 〜, put 〜)

✓ Vocabulary　下の単語の意味が確認できたら、チェックを入れましょう。

☐ add	☐ combine	☐ flour	☐ fry
☐ immediately	☐ serve	☐ vegetable	☐ pour

Unit 3 いつも何しているの?

あなたは友人に連絡しようとしています。ふだんどのような方法で連絡していますか。

 下の選択肢から連絡方法を選んで書きましょう。

(1) I usually (　　　　) my friends.
(2) Sometimes I (　　　　) my friends.＊
(3) I always use (　　　　).
(4) I never use a (　　　　).
(5) I rarely (　　　　) letters.

　　　　call　　cellphone　　landline　　text　　write　　Skype

Notes　text ▶ 携帯電話でメールする　　cellphone ▶ 携帯電話
　　　　　landline ▶ 固定電話回線

＊頻度の副詞は、ふつう主語と動詞の間に入れるが、sometimes は主語の前に置くこともできる。

Reading

アメリカの大学生活について読みましょう。 06

American college students are often busy and rarely spend much money. On weekends, what kind of activities do they do? There are many possibilities.

They often enjoy sports or events on campus. Universities usually spend a lot of money on sports and events. The events are sometimes free. Also, free concerts, parties, dinners, readings, shows and a number of events take place night and day. Many campuses have excellent museums. Student fees are often inexpensive.

The students sometimes go to the movies on weekends. Student IDs always gain great discounts on movies. And the university libraries often have a vast collection of DVDs. So students usually have many options and enjoy college life in America.

Notes
on weekends ▶ 週末に   possibility ▶ 可能性
on campus ▶ 大学構内で   take place ▶ 開催される
excellent ▶ 素晴らしい   fees ▶ 料金   inexpensive ▶ 安価な
gain great discounts on 〜 ▶ 〜を大幅に割引する
vast ▶ 膨大な   options ▶ 選択肢

本文の内容から、アメリカの大学生は週末にはどのような活動をしますか。文中の例を日本語でまとめましょう。

よくすること	
時々すること	
めったにしないこと	

現在時制と頻度の表現

● 肯定文　主語＋頻度の副詞＋動詞の現在形

頻度の副詞は主語と動詞の間に入れる（be 動詞の場合は動詞の後に）。

She exercises.　彼女は運動をします。

She often exercises on weekends.　彼女はよく週末に運動します。

● 疑問文　Do / Does ＋主語＋動詞の原形〜

Do you exercise?　あなたは運動をしますか。

Does she exercise?　彼女は運動をしますか。

頻度を聞く疑問文　How often do you 〜？

How often do you exercise?　どのような頻度で運動をしますか。

● 否定文　主語＋ do/does ＋ not ＋動詞の原形〜

I do not exercise.　私は運動をしません。

Listening & Speaking （ペアワーク）

1. YumikoとKenがそれぞれのアルバイトについて会話しています。音声を聴いて（　）に内容に合った頻度を表す表現を書き入れましょう。　　　CD 07

(1) Yumiko (　　　　) wakes up at 6.
(2) Ken (　　　　) goes to sleep before midnight
(3) Ken (　　　　) stays up late, especially on weekends.

2. 音声をもう一度聴きましょう。会話の中で2人は、How often do you ~ ? を使い頻度を尋ね合っています。答えの意味を考え、[　]から適切な日本語を選びましょう。　　　CD 07

(1) Ken: How often do you teach?
　　Yumiko: I teach twice a week.　　[週1回，週2回，月1回，年2回]
(2) Yumiko: How often do you work there (at a bakery)?
　　Ken: Every morning.　　　　　　　[毎日，毎朝，毎土曜日，毎月]

3. ペアになって頻度をたずね、表を見て答えましょう。

(1) How often do you see a movie?　どのくらいの頻度で映画を見ますか。

1回	once		week	（週に）
2回	twice	a	month	（月に）
3回	three times		year	（年に）

(2) 他の日常生活や余暇の過ごし方についてもHow often do you~? を用いて会話しましょう。下の表も使いましょう。

毎	every	morning	（朝）
		Sunday	（日曜）
		week	（週）

Writing & Speaking （ペアワーク）

1. 英語圏に新しい友人ができたと仮定して、ふだんの自分の大学生活を表すＥメールを友人に英語で書いてみましょう。[ ]内の語句や頻度の表現を必ず使いましょう。

〔weekday, weekend, stay at home, go out〕

（例）I sometimes go out on weekends.

> Dear ＿＿＿＿＿,（相手の名前）
> Thank you very much for your email about your life. Now let me tell you about my college life in Japan.
> (1) ＿＿＿＿＿＿＿＿＿＿＿＿＿＿＿＿＿＿＿＿＿＿＿＿＿＿＿＿＿＿＿.
> (2) ＿＿＿＿＿＿＿＿＿＿＿＿＿＿＿＿＿＿＿＿＿＿＿＿＿＿＿＿＿＿＿.
> (3) ＿＿＿＿＿＿＿＿＿＿＿＿＿＿＿＿＿＿＿＿＿＿＿＿＿＿＿＿＿＿＿.
> I hope to hear from you soon.
>
> Sincerely,
> ＿＿＿＿＿＿＿＿＿＿＿＿＿＿＿＿（自分の名前）

2. ペアでお互いメールを見せ合って、頻度をたずねる疑問文（How often do you ～?）を用いて内容を確認する会話をしてみましょう。

📁 Assignment

P.17 のEメールを参考に、英語であなたの1日を書きましょう。
ふだんよくすること、時々すること、あまりしないこと、を必ず入れ、
日課、アルバイトなどを含めた文章にしましょう。

👀 Let's Review! （現在時制と頻度の表現のまとめ）

- **現在時制**　日常的な習慣を表すことができる。
  - **疑問形**　Do/Does ＋主語＋動詞の原形
  - **否定形**　主語＋ do/does ＋ not ＋動詞の原形
  - **頻度の表現**　習慣を表す現在時制には頻度の表現を入れることによって、何をどの程度するかが分かる。
  - ＊頻度の表現は、ふつう主語と動詞の間に入れる。ただし be 動詞の場合は、その後に入れる。sometimes は主語の前に置くこともできる。
- **頻度の順**　頻度の順に並べると下のようになる。

| always, usually, often, sometimes, rarely, never |

100%　　　　　　　　→　　　　　　　　0%

✓ Vocabulary　下の単語の意味が確認できたら、チェックを入れましょう。

- ☐ cellphone
- ☐ on campus
- ☐ on weekends
- ☐ option
- ☐ rarely
- ☐ text
- ☐ usually
- ☐ vast

Unit 4 何を持って行きますか?

みなさんはキャンプで3日間無人島へ行くことになりました。何を持って行ったらよいでしょう。

1. 持って行くものを、何でも良いので書き出しましょう。
2. 自分の感覚で「数えられる物」(歯ブラシなど)と「数えられない物」(練り歯磨きなどの液体や粉末)に分類しましょう。
3. その分類が英語でも同じかどうかを辞書でチェックし、同じものを○で囲みましょう。

数えられる物	(歯ブラシ)
数えられない物	(練り歯磨き)

Reading

（ペアワーク）ケイコとイチローおじさんの会話を読んで、あとの問いに答えましょう。

08

Keiko is a fourth-year student. (1)She is working for her uncle's company during summer vacation.

Uncle Ichiro: Keiko, can you clean up the room?
Keiko: Uncle Ichiro, there is too much paper on the desks. Is there some other space where I can put (2)it?
Ichiro: Sure. (3)We have a lot of furniture in the office. (4)You can use the desk near the window. After cleaning up, you can go home. By the way, do you have time next Sunday? Are you busy?
Keiko: I'm sorry but I have a lot of homework, and I must get some information for my job hunting.
Ichiro: Too bad! I have two tickets to a baseball game.
Keiko: A baseball game?
Ichiro: Yes, the Tigers vs. the Giants.
Keiko: You're kidding! I'll certainly make time for the game! You know that I love baseball.
Ichiro: I thought you would. Regarding the job hunting, I'll give you some advice.
Keiko: Thank you, Uncle Ichiro!

Notes　furniture ▶ 家具　　job hunting ▶ 就職活動
you're kidding! ▶ 本当に！　　Regarding〜 ▶ 〜に関して

1. 本文中に出てくる名詞に下線を引きましょう。そして、「数えられる名詞」「数えられない名詞」をそれぞれ3つ選び、下の表に書き出しましょう。数えられる名詞については、その複数形を考えましょう。

（例）Keiko is a fourth-year student.
　　　student 数えられる名詞（単数）→ students（複数）
　　We have a lot of furniture in the office.
　　　furniture →数えられない名詞

数えられる名詞	
単数形	複数形
student	students

数えられない名詞
furniture

2. 名詞の前に付く a/an または the を「冠詞」といいます。**1.** で下線を引いた文中の名詞の前に冠詞があれば波線を引きましょう。

（例）Keiko is a fourth-year student.

3. 本文中の番号の代名詞は何・誰を指しているのでしょうか。ペアで英語の語句を探しましょう。

(1)（例）_____Keiko_____　(2) _____
(3) _____　(4) _____

4. 会話を読んだ後、もう一度音声を聴きましょう。そして、ペアになってロールプレイをしましょう。

CD 08

名　詞

名詞には「数えられる名詞」と「数えられない名詞」があります。

《名詞の前に付く語句》	
「数えられる名詞」（可算名詞）	「数えられない名詞」（不可算名詞）
単数形　冠詞（a/an または the）がつきます。	数えられない名詞の前には the, some, much, a piece of などその名詞に応じてさまざまな語句が付きます。 （例）a piece of furniture 　　　a bottle of water 　　　a cup of coffee 　　　a bag of sugar
複数形　the, some, many, a lot of, a pair of などの数量や属性を表す語句が付くことがあります。 （例）a pair of gloves 　　　（手袋などペアとなっているもの）	

the が付くとき

前後の文脈からその名詞が何を指し示すか分かる場合には the を使います。

a) すでに言及されたもの

　I bought a book. The book is for my sister.

b) 公共の施設など、文脈から特定のものだと分かるとき

　Mark hurried to the station.

c) 海や太陽などそれ1つしか存在しない物

　The earth travels around the sun.

名詞の数量を尋ねる疑問文

「数えられる名詞」の場合（many を使う）How many books do you have?
「数えられない名詞」の場合（much を使う）How much water does he have?

代　名　詞

人称代名詞は名詞の代わりに主に人を示すものです。名詞の繰り返しを避けるために使います。話している人を一人称、話し相手を二人称、話題となっている人を三人称といいます。数（単数・複数）や文中の役割によって形が変わります。（p.90 の一覧表を参照）

Listening & Speaking

以下の文の（ ）には代名詞が入ります。何が入るか考えてから音声を聴いて答えを確認してください。そして、音読練習をしましょう。

私（たち）（一人称）

(1) Manabu and I are on the same baseball team. (^{1}) are good friends. We love (^{2}) team. One day, Uncle Ichiro gave (^{3}) baseball game tickets. So (^{4}) are going to see the game.

話している相手（たち）（二人称）

(2) "Hello, Shota. Do (^{5}) have a pen? Can I borrow (^{6}) pen?"

私と話し相手以外　（三人称）

(3) Keiko studies every day because (^{7}) has a lot of homework. She often helps (^{8}) friends with homework. She is kind, so everyone likes (^{9}).

 Writing & Speaking 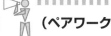 （ペアワーク）

1. Warm-up でパートナーが書いた「数えられる物」「数えられない物」から３つずつ選び、例にならって英語で書きましょう。

数えられる物	数えられない物
（例）a toothbrush	（例）a tube of toothpaste / a bottle of juice / a bag of salt
1.	1.
2.	2.
3.	3.

2. **1.** の「数えられる物」「数えられない物」から1つ選び、例にならって数量を尋ねる疑問文を書きましょう。そして、お互いに口頭で質問と答えの練習をしましょう。

（例）"books." → "How many books do you have?" － "I have three books."
　　　"toothpaste." → "How much toothpaste do you have?"
　　　　　　　　　　　－ "I have a tube of toothpaste."

(1) _____

(2) _____

📁 Assignment

自分の持ち物の中から「数えられる物」、「数えられない物」を1つずつ選び、例にならって書きましょう。

（例）I have a pair of glasses. / I have a tube of toothpaste.

1. _____
2. _____

👀 Let's Review!（名詞と代名詞のまとめ）

- 名詞は物・人・場所・抽象概念を表す。
- 名詞には「数えられる」可算名詞と「数えられない」不可算名詞があり、可算名詞には単数形と複数形がある。
- 名詞の前には冠詞（a/an や the）や数量を表すための語（a piece of など）が付くことがある。
- 人を表す人称代名詞は、文中の役割によって形が変わる。

✅ Vocabulary　下の単語の意味が確認できたら、チェックを入れましょう。

☐ advice　　☐ borrow　　☐ buy > bought　　☐ furniture
☐ information　☐ job hunting　☐ toothbrush　　☐ toothpaste

 # あなたの理想の部屋は？

部屋はその人の個性を反映するといわれています。あなたの理想の「部屋」とはどんな部屋でしょうか。

Warm-up

あなたは新しく部屋を借り、その部屋に下の物を置くことにしました。[ ]のアイコンを使って、部屋の見取り図（平面図）に家具を配置しましょう。

[bed , desk , TV-set TV , sofa , table , carpet , flower pot]

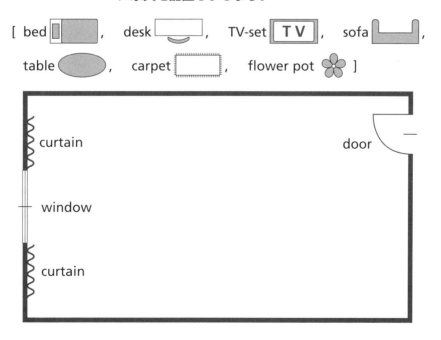

Reading

下の英文は自分の部屋を心地よい空間にデザインした人の記事です。この部屋の様子を想像しながら読みましょう。

CD 10

'Describing my dear room'

It's really great to have a room for yourself. It gives you independence and privacy.

My place has no luxury things but it is warm and attractive. It looks nice because the curtains on the windows match the bedspread. The desk is by the window. In the right corner there is a TV-set. In the opposite corner there is a sofa and a small table. A flower pot is placed near the table. On the floor I have a nice warm carpet.

I really like my room because it's comfortable. Everything in this room is precious to me.

Notes
independence ▶ 独立　luxury things ▶ ぜいたく品
attractive ▶ 魅力的な　curtains ▶ カーテン
bedspread ▶ ベッドカバー　opposite ▶ 向かい側の
comfortable ▶ 快適な　precious ▶ 貴重な

著者の部屋にある物を表にまとめましょう。

物の名前	場所
curtains	
desk	
TV-set	
sofa and table	テレビの反対側の角
flower pot	
carpet	

場所を表す表現例 − 前置詞

前置詞の後には名詞（句）が来ます。

on the desk

○の場所は以下のような表現を使えば簡単に表すことができます。

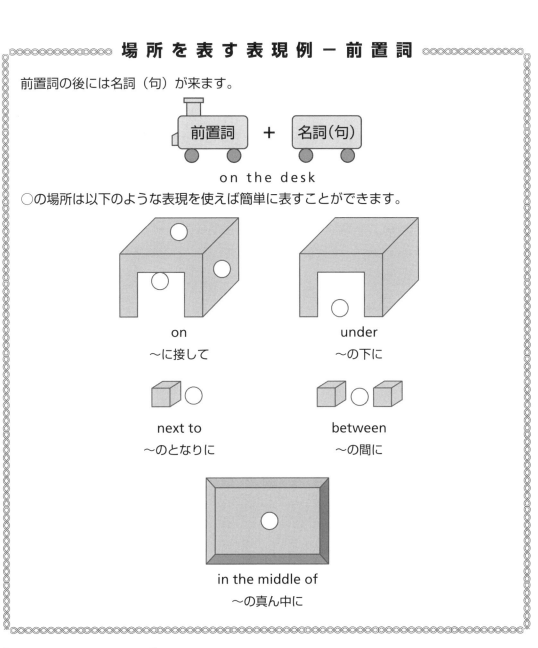

on
〜に接して

under
〜の下に

next to
〜のとなりに

between
〜の間に

in the middle of
〜の真ん中に

Listening （ペアワーク）  11

1. 音声の指示を聴いて（　）に適切な語を入れましょう。

(1) Draw two rectangles* in a row** (　　) (　　) the triangle.　　*長方形, **一列に

(2) Place a cross* (　　　) the rectangles.　　*十字形

(3) Draw two small circles (　　　) each rectangle.

(4) Place three squares* in a row (　　　) each rectangle.　　*四角形

2. 下の空欄に **1.** の音声の指示通りの図を描き、パートナーと交換して互いの絵を確認し合いましょう。

CD 11

Writing & Speaking （ペアワーク）

1. 時を表す語の前にも前置詞を使用します。次の会話の中から、時を表す前置詞を探して○で囲みましょう。

> Allen: Jane, would you like to go out with me on Sunday?
> Jane: I'd like to, but I can't. On weekends I usually get up at 9 o'clock. After breakfast I play tennis with my club mates in the morning. I have to come back by 1 o'clock to have lunch before I work part-time as a clerk in the library in the afternoon.
> Allen: Then, what about going to a movie at night?
> Jane: Well, I work until 8 o'clock in the evening, so, I don't know.

Notes mates ▶ 友達　　clerk ▶ 事務員

2. **1.** の会話の英語を使って Jane の日曜の一日を表した表を完成させましょう。

時刻	Jane の行動
at 9:00 a.m.	gets up
after breakfast	
by 1:00 p.m.	
before work	
until 8:00 p.m.	

3. **2.** の表を基に下の例の下線部を入れ替え、Jane の行動をペアになって確認し合いましょう。

（例）What does she do at 9:00 a.m.? She gets up.

時を表す前置詞

前置詞の後に来るものによって使い分けます。
at: 時刻，正午，夜半（時点、瞬間）　at 3 o'clock, at noon
on: 曜日，日　on Monday, on the 17th（the seventeenth）
in: 午前・午後，月，年（幅のある期間）　in the morning
for: 時間の長さ　for 20 minutes
by: 〜までに，until: 〜まで，during: 〜の間に

4. （　）に下の選択肢から選んだ適切な語を入れましょう。

(1) I'm planning to stay in Japan (　　) the end of this year.
(2) She gets up (　　) 7 o'clock (　　) the morning (　　) Mondays.
(3) He is planning to visit his uncle (　　) summer vacation.
(4) The meeting will start (　　) noon and last (　　) two hours.
(5) Please come back (　　) the end of this month.
　　　　　[for, by, at, until, on, in, during]

Assignment

1. Warm-up での理想の部屋の絵を「場所を表す前置詞」を使って英語で描写してみましょう。次に絵を示しながら説明しましょう。

(例) table	There is a table in front of the window.
desk	
bed	
TV-set	
flower pot	
carpet	

2. 今度は、ある日のあなたの行動を朝起きてから寝るまでの順に従って前置詞 at / in / after / by / before / until などを使って説明しましょう。

（例）7 a.m.	I get up at 7 a.m.

[have lunch, go shopping, work part-time, take a bath, go to bed,]
（昼食をとる　　買物にいく　　バイトをする　　お風呂に入る　　寝る）

Let's Review! （前置詞のまとめ）

● 「場所を表す前置詞」

The library is at the end of this street. 前置詞の後は名詞（句）
at 〜に　（比較的狭い場所）at the end of 〜の端に
on 〜に接して（〜の上に）on the wall 壁に
in 〜の中に（広がりのある場所の中）in the middle of 〜の真ん中に
over 〜の上方に（接触していない）under 〜の下に（接触・非接触とも）
around 〜の周囲に　by 〜のそばに　next to 〜の隣に

● 「時を表す前置詞」

We had lunch at noon today. 前置詞の後は名詞（句）
at: 時刻，正午，夜半（時点）at 3 o'clock, at noon
on: 曜日，日　on Monday, on the 17th (the seventeenth)
in: 午前，月，年（幅のある期間）in the evening, in April, in 2013
after 〜の後　before 〜の前　around およそ〜　during 〜の間

Vocabulary　下の単語の意味が確認できたら、チェックを入れましょう。

☐ attractive　　☐ clerk　　☐ comfortable　　☐ curtains
☐ independence　☐ luxury　　☐ opposite　　☐ precious

Unit 6 目指そう！ 健康生活

あなたは規則正しい生活を送っていますか。もっと運動すべきだ，食生活を見直す必要がある，早寝早起きを心がけるべきだ・・・心当たりはありますか。

 （ペアワーク）

ペアになって、すごろく質問ゲームをしましょう。
順番にサイコロを転がし、出た目の数だけ進んで、たどりついたマスに書いてある質問をパートナーにしましょう。パートナーはその質問に答えましょう。

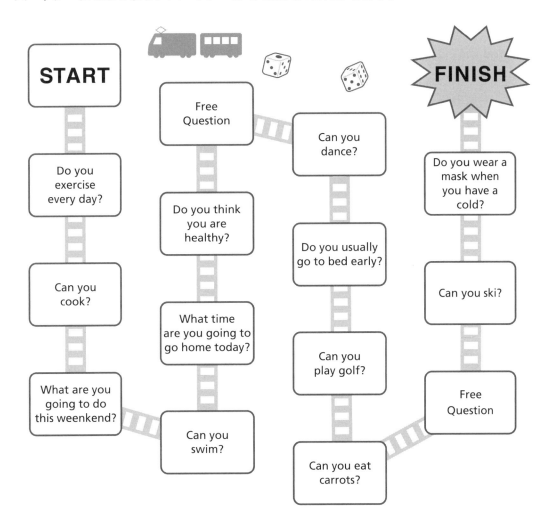

Reading

次の英文を読んで、後の問いに答えましょう。

How to Stay Healthy

It is often said that health is better than wealth, but it is difficult to stay healthy. Some students are not interested in their health and become sick. So, I'll give you some advice about how to stay healthy.

First, you should exercise. You don't have to play soccer or go to the gym. You should do simple exercises such as walking or jogging every day.

Second, you should have a well-balanced diet: fruit, vegetables, meat, fish, beans, milk, bread, rice, etc. I know many of you, especially girls, go on a diet to lose weight, but you must not eat too little.

Third, you should sleep well. You must not stay up late at night. You should go to bed early every day.

Notes
health is better than wealth ▶ 健康は富に勝る
exercise ▶ 運動(する)　well-balanced diet ▶ バランスのとれた食事
go on a diet ▶ ダイエットする　lose weight ▶ 減量する
stay up late ▶ 遅くまで起きている

1. should / don't have to / must not の8カ所を○で囲みましょう。

2. 下の表を完成させましょう。

すべきこと (should)	しなくてもよいこと (don't have to)	してはいけないこと (must not)
・exercise	・	・
・	・	・
・		
・		
・		

助動詞

助動詞は、動詞の原形と共に使います。
　can（～できる）will（～でしょう，～するつもり）should（～すべき）
　may（～するかもしれない，～してもよい）must/have to（～しなければならない）
　must not（～してはいけない）don't have to（～する必要はない）
　　＊can の過去形→could　　＊will の過去形→would

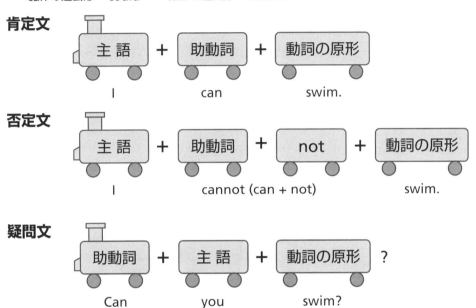

 Listening & Speaking （ペアワーク）  13

1. 音声を聴いて（　）に単語を書き入れましょう。

(1) (　　) (　　) turn on the air conditioner?
エアコンをつけていただけませんか。

(2) (　　) (　　) help me with my homework?
宿題を手伝ってくれない？

(3) (　　) (　　) visit your office this afternoon?
今日の午後、研究室に伺ってもよろしいですか。

(4) (　　) (　　) use your cellphone?
携帯電話を借りてもいい？

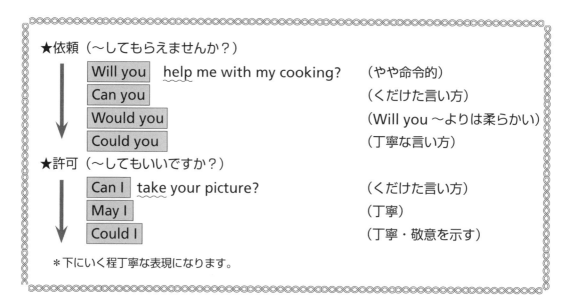

2. それぞれのイラストに対応する英語の表現を下から選び、（　）に記号を書き入れましょう。その後、健康を維持するために、(1) すべきこと、(2) しなくてもよいこと、(3) してはいけないと思うことを、下の表現を使ってペアで話しましょう。

( ) gain weight　　　　　　　( ) sleep well　　　　　　( ) eat between meals
( ) have a well-balanced diet　( ) go on a diet　　　　　( ) eat fast food
( ) exercise regularly　　　　 ( ) do a workout

(1) I should _____.

(2) I don't have to _____.

(3) I must not _____.

Writing & Speaking （ペアワーク）

1. あなた自身のことについて次の表を埋め、ペアで発表し合いましょう。

できること (can)	I
できないこと (can't)	I
しなければならないこと (must / have to)	I
してはいけないこと (must not / mustn't)	I
明日しようと思うこと (will)	I
〜するかもしれないと思うこと (may)	I

2. あなたは健康アドバイザーです。
パートナーに次の質問をし、下記の問診票を完成させましょう。

1	Do you smoke?	Yes / No
2	Do you drink alcohol every day?	Yes / No
3	Do you usually have breakfast?	Yes / No
4	Do you eat a lot?	Yes / No
5	Do you usually eat between meals?	Yes / No
6	Do you prefer meat to vegetables?	Yes / No
7	Do you take much sugar in your coffee/tea?	Yes / No
8	Do you want to go on a diet?	Yes / No
9	Do you exercise regularly?	Yes / No
10	Do you stay up late at night?	Yes / No

Assignment (ペアワーク)

問診票を基に、健康を保つ方法についてパートナーにアドバイスをしてあげましょう。文章の続きを完成させた後、口頭で伝えましょう。その際、p.33の助動詞を使いましょう。

（例）You should have breakfast.

I'll give you some advice about how to stay healthy.

First, you _____

_____

Second, you _____

_____

Third, you _____

_____

Let's Review! （助動詞のまとめ）

- **肯定文**　　I can play the drums.　私はドラムを演奏できる。
- **否定文**　　I cannot play the drums.　私はドラムを演奏できない。
- **疑問文**　　Can you play the drums?　ドラムを演奏できますか。

↓

＊動詞は必ず原形

・It will be sunny tomorrow.　明日は晴れるだろう。

・You should tell the truth.　あなたは真実を言うべきだ。

・She may be right.　彼女は正しいかもしれない。

・I have to leave now.　もう帰らなければならない。

・You must not cheat on the test.　テストでカンニングしてはいけない。

・You don't have to wear a tie.　ネクタイをする必要はない。

Vocabulary

下の単語の意味が確認できたら、チェックを入れましょう。

- ☐ bread
- ☐ eat between meals
- ☐ exercise
- ☐ gain weight
- ☐ go on a diet
- ☐ healthy
- ☐ lose weight
- ☐ stay up late

Unit 7 旅に出よう

どこか旅に出かけたくなるときがありますか。そこで、どんなことをしてみたいですか。

Warm-up あなたにぴったりの旅行先はどこでしょう。
次の Yes/No チャートの質問に答えてみつけましょう。

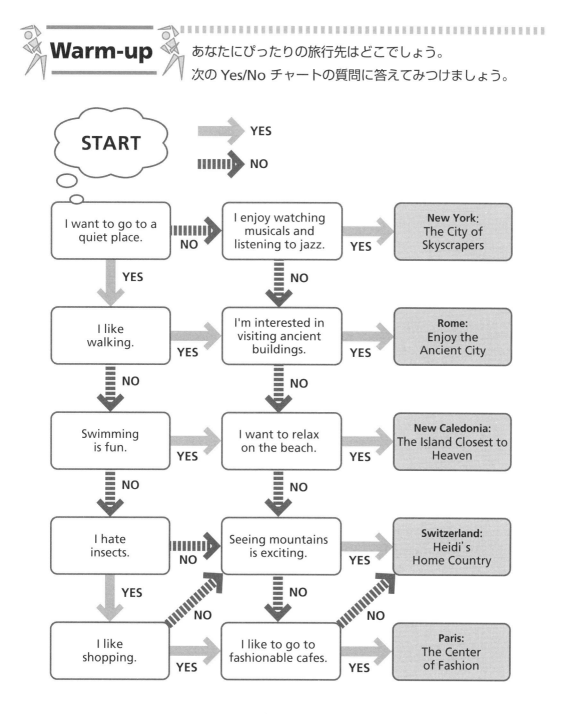

Reading

 （ペアワーク）以下の英文を読んで問いに答えましょう。 14

Manabu likes to travel around Japan. There are many beautiful places to visit. Among them, he believes that Hokkaido is worth visiting again. He is making a plan to visit Hokkaido in summer. During spring vacation, he worked hard to save money. Almost every day, he worked at a convenience store. So he saved enough to go to Hokkaido.

Manabu plans to go by train. He likes taking trains. However, Hokkaido is a long way to go. He asked Yuko to lend him some travel books. By reading these books, he may find a good way to travel around. He wants to eat seafood and see the beautiful landscapes there. For him, eating local food is one of the joys of travel. Also, he is interested in taking pictures. He learned how to take good photos. He is sure he will have a wonderful trip.

Notes worth ~ing ▶ ～する価値がある　save money ▶ お金をためる
enough ▶ 十分な　landscape ▶ 風景

1. to ＋動詞原形には下線を、動詞 +ing には波線を引きましょう。

2. 下の文の意味をペアで考えて、日本語で書きましょう。

(1) There are many beautiful places to visit.
_____

(2) Hokkaido is a long way to go by train.
_____

(3) By reading these books, he may find a good way to travel around Hokkaido.
_____

3. 次の質問にペアで答えを考えて日本語で書き入れましょう。

マナブが好きなことは何ですか。	
マナブはユウコに何を頼みましたか。	
マナブは春休みに何をしたのでしょう。	
マナブはいつ北海道へ行くつもりですか。	

＜動名詞：動詞原形 -ing＞ ＜to 不定詞：to + 動詞原形＞

●不定詞・動名詞の名詞用法

「動名詞」は動詞の性質を持ちつつ名詞の働きをします。「to 不定詞」も名詞の働きをします。

主語として

Reading books is fun. / To read books is fun.　本を読むことは楽しい。

動詞の補語または目的語として

I like reading books. / I like to read books.　私は本を読むことが好きだ。

前置詞の目的語として

By reading books, I can learn a lot.
本を読むことによって、私はたくさん学ぶことができる。

●不定詞の形容詞用法　（名詞を修飾する用法）

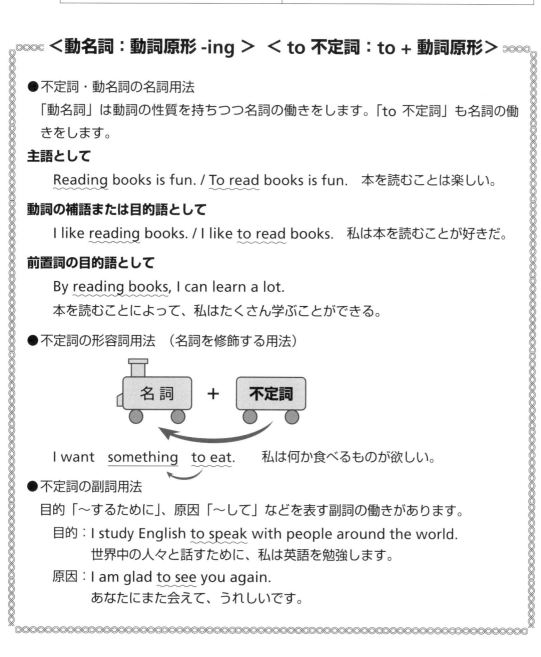

I want　something　to eat.　私は何か食べるものが欲しい。

●不定詞の副詞用法

目的「〜するために」、原因「〜して」などを表す副詞の働きがあります。

　目的：I study English to speak with people around the world.
　　　　世界中の人々と話すために、私は英語を勉強します。

　原因：I am glad to see you again.
　　　　あなたにまた会えて、うれしいです。

1.

音声を聴いて、次の会話文の（　）に単語を書き入れましょう。そしてペアになり音読練習をしましょう。

Manabu: Hi, Yuko. How are you?
Yuko: Oh, hi. I'm OK.
Manabu: I want to (¹　　　　) you a favor. Can I borrow your travel books on Hokkaido?
Yuko: No problem. You really like (²　　　　)!
Manabu: To (³　　　　) is to (⁴　　　　) something. We meet many people on a journey. It is exciting to (⁵　　　　) new people. I enjoy (⁶　　　　) with them. Also, Hokkaido is worth (⁷　　　　) again. It's a beautiful place.
Yuko: Well, I understand. Your dream is to (⁸　　　　) a tour guide, right? I'll lend you some books on traveling. By (⁹　　　　) these books, you'll learn a lot of things.
Manabu: Thank you! I need something interesting to (¹⁰　　　　) on the long journey. Now, I must save money to (¹¹　　　　) to Hokkaido.
Yuko: I'm good at (¹²　　　　) pictures. I'll give you some tips on how to (¹³　　　　) good photos.
Manabu: Thank you! I am happy to (¹⁴　　　　) good friends like you!

Notes　a favor ▶ お願い　discover ▶ 発見する
journey ▶ 旅　tips ▶ コツ

2. 旅行に行くとしたらどこへ行きたいですか。また、会話文を参考にして、してみたいこと、興味があることを不定詞または動名詞を使って 2 つの英文で書き表しましょう。そしてパートナーに話しましょう。

・行きたい場所　（例）Rome

_____

・そこでしてみたいこと・興味があること
（例）I want to visit the Colosseum. / I'm interested in eating pizza.

(1) _____

(2) _____

Writing & Speaking （ペアワーク）

マナブのプロフィールをみて、不定詞か動名詞を使って英文で書きましょう。そしてペアでお互いに音読しましょう。

マナブくんのプロフィール
・旅行が好き
・趣味は野球を見ること
・英語を話すことが得意
・海外旅行に行くために働いている
・写真を撮ることに興味がある

（例）：He likes traveling.

_____
_____
_____
_____

☐ Assignment

Reading と **Listening** で使われている文章を参考に、自分のことや、してみたいことを不定詞または動名詞を使って書きましょう。

I like _____.

_____ is exciting.

I enjoy _____.

My dream is _____.
By _____ , I'll learn a lot of things.
I need something interesting to _____ on the long journey.
I must save money to _____.
I am good at _____ ing _____.
I will give you some tips on how to _____.
I am happy to _____.

Let's Review! （不定詞と動名詞のまとめ）

● to 不定詞：to + 動詞の原形
「to 不定詞」は動詞の意味を持ちながら、「〜すること」（名詞用法）・「〜するための」（形容詞用法）・「〜するために」「〜して」など（副詞用法）の働きをする。

名詞用法

To read books is fun.

I like to read books.

形容詞用法

I want something to eat .

副詞用法

I study English to speak with people around the world.

I am glad to see you again.

● 動名詞：　動詞の原形 -ing
「動名詞」は動詞と名詞の性質を持っている。意味は「〜すること」。

Reading books is fun.

I like reading books.

Vocabulary　下の単語の意味が確認できたら、チェックを入れましょう。

☐ a favor　　☐ discover　　☐ enough　　☐ exciting

☐ glad　　　☐ insect　　　☐ landscape　☐ quiet

☐ save money　☐ worth ~ing

Unit 8 パーティーを開こう！

今日はパーティーを開きます。
今から楽しみです。

 イラストの人物の動作を説明している語を選択肢の中から選び、（　）に書き入れましょう。

1. The woman is (　　　　) for the party.
　　女性はパーティーの準備をしている。

2. The (　　　　) baby
　　泣いている赤ちゃん

3. The boy (　　　　) a present in a box
　　箱に入ったプレゼントを持っている少年

holding,　preparing,　crying

Reading (ペアワーク)

次の電話の会話を読んで、問いに答えましょう。

Ken: Hello?

Mary: Hello, Ken. This is Mary.

Ken: Oh, hi. How was your vacation?

Mary: I didn't go anywhere because I couldn't get airplane tickets. So I went to the library and checked out some books instead.

Ken: What're you reading now?

Mary: I'm reading *A History of Time*. It's very difficult, but I wanted to understand how the universe began. What're you doing?

Ken: Well, I'm preparing dinner.

Mary: What're you cooking?

Ken: I'm baking some potatoes and grilling a huge salmon.

Mary: Are you going to have a party tonight?

Ken: Yeah, Tom and his friend are supposed to come here. Do you want to join us?

Mary: I'd love to. Thank you!

Ken: Okay, see you later.

Notes check out ▶ （本などを）借りる　instead ▶ その代わりに
how the universe began ▶ どのようにして宇宙が始まったのか
be supposed to *do* ▶ 〜することになっている

1. 〈be 動詞〉+〈動詞+ -ing〉は「～しているところである」という意味を表します。〈動詞+ -ing〉の 7 つの箇所に丸をつけましょう。そして、Mary と Ken の行動について、下の空欄を日本語で埋め、ペアになって答えを確認し合いましょう。

Mary が今していること

```
メアリーは図書館に行った。今は
```

Ken が今していること

```
ケンは今日パーティーを開くので、
```

2. 例を参考にし、表中の動詞を使って〈be 動詞〉+〈動詞+ -ing〉を用いた英文を作りましょう。主語はあらかじめ指定してあります。また、主語によって変化する〈be 動詞〉の形に注意しましょう。

〈動詞+ -ing〉	意味	英文
reading	読んでいる	例：Mary is reading a novel.
doing	～をしている	I
preparing	準備をしている	They
cooking	料理をしている	Ken
baking	オーブンで焼いている	My mother
grilling	網で焼いている	We

3. Reading の会話の内容を確認しましょう。そして、音声を聴きましょう。さらにペアになり、大きな声を出して会話の練習をしましょう。 CD 16

Hello.
What're you doing?

Oh, hi...
I'm -ing...

現在分詞の表すもの

〈動詞＋ -ing〉を現在分詞と呼びます。現在分詞は「～しているところである」という進行中の動作を表すため、現在進行形に用いられます。

主語 が～しているところである

I　　am　　playing　　the　　guitar.

また、名詞の前後に置けば、名詞を修飾する形容詞（句）の働きもします。

～している 名詞

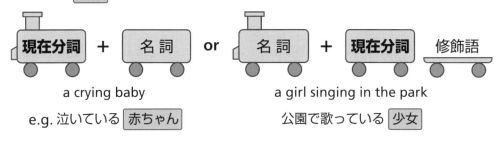

a crying baby　　　　　　　a girl singing in the park
e.g. 泣いている 赤ちゃん　　公園で歌っている 少女

Listening

音声を聴いて、下の選択肢から適切な語を（　）に書き入れ、文の意味を考えましょう。

CD 17

(1) Ken and Mary are (　　　　) on the phone right now.

(2) Ken is the person (　　　　) a party in his house.

(3) Ken is (　　　　) the food, so he is (　　　　) vegetables and fish.

(4) The guests (　　　　) to the party are Tom and his friend.

(5) The person (　　　　) the party is Mary, because she doesn't have any plans.

---

coming,　　preparing,　　joining,　　talking,　　cooking,　　throwing

Writing & Speaking （ペアワーク）

登場人物：Ken, Mary, Their mother

A.
Look at the girl standing by the big tree.
Her name is Mary. What's she doing?

B.
She is preparing for a barbecue party with her mother. Her brother grilling beef steaks looks very busy.

1. 絵の人物が現在何をしているところか、ペアになってパートナーと一緒に考えましょう。〈動詞＋ -ing〉を使った英文を作成し、空欄に記入しましょう。「吹き出し」を参考にしてください。

> A: Look at the girl... Her name is Mary.
>   What's she doing?
> B: She is –ing... Her brother...
>
> A:
>
> B:

2. ペアで作成した会話をクラス内で発表しましょう。

3. **Warm-up** の **1.** ～ **3.** の絵をもう一度見て、英語で表現しましょう。

(1) 女性はパーティーの準備をしているところだ。（準備をする：prepare）

The woman _____.

(2) 部屋には泣いている赤ちゃんがいる。（～がいる：there is ～）

There is _____.

(3) プレゼントを持っている少年はトムだ。（～を持っている：hold）

The boy _____.

📁 Assignment （ペアワーク）

The boy washing dishes in the kitchen is Ken. The woman vacuuming the carpet in the living room is Mary. She is his sister. The baby on the couch is their cousin, John.

訳 台所でお皿を洗っている少年はケンです。リビングのカーペットに掃除機をかけている女性はメアリーです。彼女はケンのお姉さんです。ソファの上の赤ちゃんはいとこのジョンです。

上の日本語とその英文を参考にし、2人一組で、ケンとメアリーの役になって、短い会話を作成しましょう。そして、それぞれの役を演じましょう。

Ken:
Mary:
Ken:
Mary:

👓 Let's Review! （現在分詞のまとめ）

● **現在進行形（〜しているところである）**　be 動詞＋現在分詞

The boy is playing the violin in the room.
その少年は部屋でバイオリンを弾いているところだ。

● ☐ を説明するとき（〜している ☐ ）

The walking woman is Ken's sister.
歩いている女性はケンのお姉さんだ。

There are a lot of people working in the kitchen.
台所で働いているたくさんの人たちがいる。

✅ Vocabulary　下の単語の意味が確認できたら、チェックを入れましょう。

☐ couch　☐ difficult　☐ dish　☐ guest　☐ hold
☐ huge　☐ plan　☐ vacation　☐ vacuum

Unit 9 割れた窓？

野球のボールが当たったのでしょうか、それとも誰かが割ったのでしょうか。窓が壊されています。

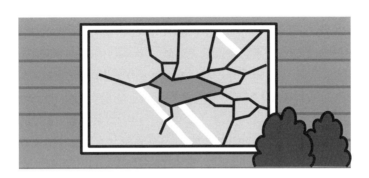

Warm-up

（ ）に適切な言葉を書き入れて、絵の状況を説明しましょう。

1.

Tom　　　　　　　　　cup

Tom は cup を壊した　　cup は（　　　　　　）

2.

Jane　　　　　　　　　Tom

Jane は Tom を（　　　　　　）　Tom は Jane に（　　　　　　　）

Reading

Kevin はおしゃれな大学生です。
下の会話文を読んで問いに答えましょう。

Kevin: Guess what? I was chosen Best Dresser of the Year in the college!
Jane: Hey, that's great! Who were the judges?
Kevin: There is a special committee to choose the winner of the prize, and they chose me!
Jane: Congratulations! Did they give you anything for it?
Kevin: Yeah, I was given a free ticket to ── Hawaii!

....

Jane: Hi, how was the vacation? How did you find the food in Hawaii?
Kevin: Oh, I loved it. I had a Loco Moco for lunch almost every day.
Jane: Loco Moco? What's that?
Kevin: Loco Moco is Hawaii's original homemade fast food and can be found just about everywhere.

Notes　judge ▶ 審査員　committee ▶ 委員会　prize ▶ 賞

1. 会話の中から過去分詞とその単語の原形を探して○で囲み、選んだ単語を用いて下の表を完成させましょう。

現在形	過去形	過去分詞
選ぶ（　　　　）	選んだ（chose）	（　　　　）
与える（　　　　）	与えた（gave）	（　　　　）
見つける（　　　　）	見つけた（found）	（　　　　）

2. 会話の内容に基づいて、下の表を完成させましょう。

委員会は	ベストドレッサー	を選んで	賞品	を与えた
Kevinは		に（　　　）		を（　　　）

過去分詞の表すもの

過去分詞は、①「～された」のような受け身、②「～してしまった」のような動作の完了状態の意味を表すため、受動態や完了形に用いられます。

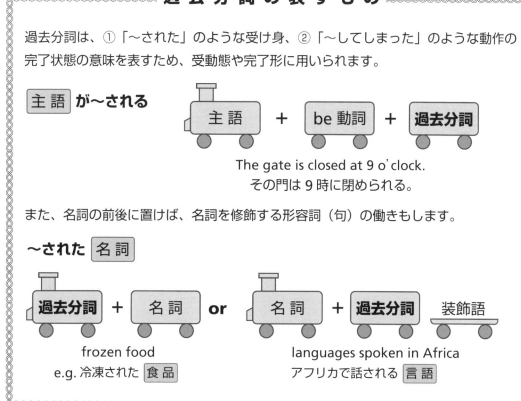

また、名詞の前後に置けば、名詞を修飾する形容詞（句）の働きもします。

 **Listening** 音声を聴いて、下の選択肢から適切な語を（ ）に書き入れ、文の意味を考えましょう。　CD 19

(1) A famous anime movie will be (　　　) in this theater next week.

(2) Mary is very beautiful, so she is (　　　) to win the contest.

(3) This is the novel (　　　) by a young university student.

(4) If you use this (　　　) card, you don't need to carry cash in the park.

(5) I went to the supermarket to buy (　　　) foods because they were on sale.

---

frozen,　　expected,　　prepaid,　　shown,　　written

Writing & Speaking （ペアワーク）

1. 日本語を参考にして、例にならって言い換えましょう。ペアで確認し合い、下線にその文を書きましょう。

（例） Ⓐ Mary played the piano.
Ⓑ The piano was played by Mary.

(1) Ⓐ My mother cooks dinner.
Ⓑ Dinner _____ .
（夕食は母によって作られる。）

(2) Ⓐ Tom broke the window.
Ⓑ The window _____ .
（その窓はトムに壊された。）

(3) Ⓐ The police caught the criminal.
Ⓑ The criminal _____ .
（その犯人は警察に捕らえられた。）

2. 例にならって「これは～だ」という文に言い換えましょう。ペアで確認し合い、下線にその文を書きましょう。

Ⓐ This computer is used by David.
（例） Ⓑ This is the computer used by David.

(1) Ⓐ Dinner is cooked by my mother.

Ⓑ This is the dinner _____.

(2) Ⓐ The window was broken by Tom.

Ⓑ This is the window _____.

(3) Ⓐ These flowers were planted by kindergarten kids.

Ⓑ These are the flowers _____.

3. Warm-up 1. ～ 2. の絵をもう一度見て、英語で表現してみましょう。

(1) トムはそのカップを壊した。(壊す：break)

Tom _____.

そのカップはトムに壊された。

The cup _____.

(2) Jane はトムを驚かせた。(驚かす：surprise)

Jane _____.

トムは Jane に驚かされた。

Tom _____.

📁 Assignment　怪盗ルパン（Lupin the phantom thief）についての話を読みましょう。

Everybody knows 'Lupin the phantom thief.' One day, when he was about to rob ABC bank, a guard saw him. Police officers finally caught Lupin and took him to a police station.

訳 誰でも怪盗ルパンを知っている。ある日、ABC 銀行に強盗に入ろうとした時、警備員が彼を見つけた。警察官たちはとうとう彼を捕まえて、警察署に連行した。

下の訳をヒントにして、怪盗ルパンの立場で（ルパンを主語にして）この話を英語で説明してみましょう。

_____

_____

訳 怪盗ルパンは皆に知られている。ある日、ABC 銀行に強盗に入ろうとした時、彼は警備員に見つけられた。彼はとうとう警察官たちに捕まえられて、警察署に連行された。

👁 Let's Review! （過去分詞のまとめ）

● **受け身（〜される）**：be 動詞 ＋ **過去分詞** （＋ by する人・物）

　　The teacher was respected by the students.
　　その先生は学生に尊敬されていた。

● ☐ を説明するとき（〜された ☐ ）

　　The blocked <u>area</u> was full of snow.

　　封鎖された区域は雪でいっぱいだった

　　This is the <u>engine</u> driven by steam.

　　これは蒸気で動かされているエンジンだ

☑ Vocabulary　下の単語の意味が確認できたら、チェックを入れましょう。

☐ choose　　☐ committee　☐ expect　　☐ frozen

☐ judge　　　☐ prepaid　　 ☐ prize　　　☐ respect

スポーツをしよう

あなたはこれまで、どんなスポーツをしたことがありますか。そしてそれを今もしていますか。

 （ペアワーク）

1. あなたが「過去にしたスポーツ」と「過去から現在までしているスポーツ」を下から選んで、表の中に書き入れましょう。

過去（今はしていない）	過去〜現在（今もしている）

(A) baseball basketball rugby soccer tennis volleyball
(B) archery judo karate kendo sumo track and field
(C) bowling curling jogging skiing skating swimming

＊「〜をする」と表現するとき、(A) の球技は play 〜、(B) のボールを使わないものは do 〜、(C) の ing がつくものは、go 〜か ing なしの動詞形を使います。

2. ペアになって、上の表を確認し合いましょう。そして自分がしたことのあるスポーツについて、始めた時期やきっかけを日本語で話し合いましょう。

Reading  会話文を読んで、下の問いに答えましょう。 20

Mari: Have you ever seen a curling game?

Manabu: Yes, I have. I saw one on TV last week. It was exciting and looked like a lot of fun.

Mari: Today curling is getting popular in Japan. I started curling when I was at high school. Now I belong to the college curling club.

Manabu: Wow, sounds great! So, you have curled for...

Mari: For about three years, but I've never won a game.

Manabu: What is most interesting about curling?

Mari: Well, curling is very safe and easy to try. Even beginners can enjoy it a lot. But, to tell the truth, there are not many curlers in Japan, so I hope to make the team for the next winter Olympics!

Note make the team ▶ チームの一員になる

1. マリについて、下の表を日本語で完成させましょう。

カーリングを始めた時期	
カーリングをしている期間	
試合に勝った回数	

2. 「過去のこと」（過去形）と「過去から現在までのこと」（have ＋過去分詞形）を表現している文を、それぞれあと２つ書き出しましょう。

「過去」

I saw one on TV last week.

- _____
- _____

「過去～現在」

Have you ever seen a curling game?

- _____
- _____

現在完了

現在完了形は、過去から現在までつながっている時間帯を表します。次の図の ⬜ の部分、つまり「過去～現在」のでき事を表現するときに使います。

「過去」I lived in Osaka in 1999.　　　「現在」I live in Osaka now.

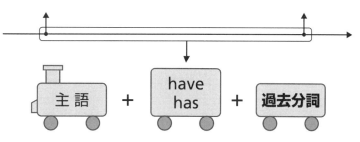

「過去～現在」I have lived in Osaka since 1999.
私は1999年以来、大阪に住んでいる。

否定文：主語＋ have [has] ＋ not ＋過去分詞 ～．
　　　　She **has not lived** here for a long time.

疑問文：Have [Has] ＋主語＋過去分詞 ～？
　　　　Have you **lived** here for a long time?

＊短縮形：I have → I've　She has → She's　have not → haven't　has not → hasn't

 Listening 音声を聴いて、（ ）に単語を書き入れましょう。 21

(1) I (　　)(　　) soccer since I was seven years old.

(2) (　　) never (　　) Kendo before.

(3) My brother (　　)(　　) skiing for a week with his friend.

(4) (　　) you ever (　　) to Australia?

(5) My mother will come back soon. (　　)(　　) to the nearby shop.

Speaking （ペアワーク）

ペアになって、太字の部分を下の語句と入れ替えてロールプレイをしましょう。

> A: Have you ever **played basketball**?
> B: Yes, I've **played it for five years**.
> A: Have you been to **Yoyogi National Gymnasium**?
> B: Yes, I've been there **three times**. It's a holy place for **basketball**.

Notes have been to ▶ 〜へ行ったことがある　holy place ▶ 聖地

	スポーツ	期　間	場　所	回　数
①	play baseball	for six months	Koshien Stadium	many times
②	do judo	since high school	Kodokan	once

Writing

1. それぞれの図を参考にして、日本語を表す英文を完成させましょう。

(1) My father was busy yesterday.　　He is still busy.

My father ＿＿＿＿＿ busy since yesterday.　父は昨日から多忙です。

(2) I lost my wallet a few days ago.　I don't have it now.

I ＿＿＿＿＿ my wallet.　財布を失くしてしまいました。

(3) I traveled to Okinawa.　　I have a memory of it now.

I ＿＿＿＿＿ to Okinawa.　沖縄へ旅行したことがあります。

(4) John came to Japan ten years ago.　He is still in Japan.

John _____ in Japan for ten years.　ジョンが来日して 10 年になります。

---

2. （ ）内の語句を加えて、英文を現在完了形に変えましょう

(1) He uses this PC. (since 2010)
　　彼はこのパソコンを 2010 年から使っています。
　　_____

(2) The train doesn't leave. (yet)
　　電車はまだ出発していません。
　　_____

(3) Do you see this picture? (before)
　　以前にこの絵を見たことがありますか。
　　_____

---

3. 下線部に注意して、[ ]内の語句のうち正しいものを○で囲みましょう。

(1) She [goes / went / has gone] to the party yesterday.

(2) Mari and I [know / knew / have known] each other for many years.

(3) I can't find my key. [Do you see / Did you see / Have you seen] it?

(4) James [comes / came / has come] to Japan in 2005.

(5) Haruna [lives / lived / has lived] in Kobe since she was born.

Assignment (ペアワーク)

マナブのプロフィールをみて、英文を書いてみましょう。
そしてペアでお互いに音読しましょう。

マナブくんのプロフィール
・京都に5年間在住
・柔道歴3年、試合（match）に勝ったことがない
・北海道旅行2回、海外旅行（travel abroad）は未経験

例：He has lived in Kyoto for five years.

_____

_____

_____

_____

_____

_____

_____

Let's Review! （現在完了形のまとめ）(have ＋ 過去分詞)

● I have worked at a restaurant for two years.
  2年間レストランで働いている。
  [継続] を表す語：for「～の間」 since「～以来」など

● Have you ever seen a panda? — No, I never have.
  パンダを見たことがありますか。　いいえ、一度もありません。
  [経験] を表す語：ever「今までに」 never「一度も～ない」 before「以前に」
  　　　　　　　once「かつて、1回」 three times「3回」など

● We have already spent all our money.
  私たちはすでにお金を全て使ってしまった。
  [完了・結果] を表す語：already「すでに」 yet「（疑問文で）もう～、（否定文で）まだ～（ない）」など

Vocabulary

下の単語の意味が確認できたら、チェックを入れましょう。

☐ do judo　　☐ for ten years　　☐ go skiing　　☐ play soccer
☐ since 2005　☐ three times　　☐ win a match

Unit 11 フリマでお買い物

フリーマーケット（flea market: ノミの市）にはさまざまなものが売られています。あなたはどんなものを買ってみたいですか。

Warm-up

1. あなたはフリーマーケットに行ったことがありますか。どんな品物が売られているのか考えましょう。

2. あなたは大学主催のフリーマーケットに3点出品することにしました。出品するものをイラストで描きましょう。

（例）

1.	2.	3.

3. あなたの商品の特徴を表す言葉を例にならって英語で書き入れましょう。

商品	色	状態
T-shirt	white	good / almost new

大きさ・重さ	材質	その他
L size / light	cotton / wool	made in the U.S.

4. リストの言葉を用いて、あなたの商品を英語で簡単に説明しましょう。
（例）「新品のTシャツ」a new T-shirt /「古くて赤い本」an old red book　など

 **Reading** 以下の英文を読んで問いに答えましょう。 22

Going to a Flea Market

Last week, I went to a flea market with one of my friends. First, we went to a stall selling T-shirts, jeans, and clothes. I found two T-shirts that I liked—one was yellow, and the other one was blue. I wanted to buy both, but the blue one was too small. I decided to buy the yellow one. My friend found a green woolen jacket. It was the oldest one in the stall, but he liked it very much. The seller reduced the price by 50 percent so we could buy them more cheaply.

Next, we visited another stall selling antique goods. I found a cute teddy bear made in England. It was cuter than any other teddy bear, but it was the most expensive one. The seller recommended a small bear to me. It was much cheaper than the other one. In the end, I decided to buy the one he recommended.

Notes stall ▶ 露店　reduce ▶（値段を）下げる
by 50 percent ▶ 50％分（差を表す）

1. 私と友人はそれぞれ何を買いましたか。日本語で具体的に（色・サイズなど）説明しましょう。

私	友人

2. 本文の中で形容詞が含まれている箇所を見つけ、下線を引きましょう。

3. 商品を比べている箇所を見つけ、波線を引きましょう。

4. 3. で引いた波線の中から形容詞を抜き出し、それぞれの原級・比較級・最上級を下の表に書きましょう。次に、表の (1) 〜 (3) の空欄をそれぞれ書き入れましょう。

原　級	比較級 [-er]	最上級 [the -est]
（例）small	smaller	the smallest
(1) big		
(2)		the best
(3)	less	

形 容 詞 ・ 比 較 表 現

〈形容詞〉

人やモノ［＝名詞］の「性質・状態・質・量」を説明します。

例）a red pencil.　赤鉛筆　/　The pencil is red.　鉛筆は赤色だ

〈比較表現〉

人やモノの「性質・状態・質・量」を比べるときに使います。その際、形容詞の形を以下のように変化させます。

● 「〜と同じくらい…」（原級）：

　　A is　＋　as 形容詞 as　＋　B (is).

● 「〜より…」（比較級）：

　　A is　＋　- er /more 形容詞　＋　than B (is).

● 「〜の中で最も…」（最上級）：

　　A is　＋　the - est /most 形容詞　＋　in [場所]. / of [all / 数字].

＊長いつづりの形容詞の比較・最上級では more / the most 形容詞を使用します。

＊比較の文では、than 以下が省略される場合もあります。
＊ as 〜 as の文で否定文のときは、not so 形容詞 as という場合もあります。
＊比較・最上級には不規則変化するものがあります。
（例）good (well)-better-best, bad (ill)-worse-worst など

Listening

音声を聴いて、次の会話文の（ ）に単語を書き入れましょう。また、ヒロミが何を買ったのか考えましょう。

CD 23

Sales Clerk: Hello, how can I help you?
 Hiromi: Hello, I'm looking for a shirt.
Sales Clerk: Sure. What kind of shirt would you like?
 Hiromi: Can I have a look at this (¹) (²)?
Sales Clerk: Here you are.
 Hiromi: Let me see... Oh, it's made of cotton. And it's not (³) (⁴) (⁵) the other shirts.
Sales Clerk: That's right! This is (⁶) (⁷).
 Hiromi: Really? It looks (⁸)! How much is it?
Sales Clerk: It's (⁹) yen.
 Hiromi: Mmm... Could you give me a discount?
Sales Clerk: Well..., how about (¹⁰) yen?
 Hiromi: That would be (¹¹). OK, I'll take it.
Sales Clerk: Thank you very much!

Writing & Speaking （ペアワーク）

1. 下のイラストを、それぞれの指示に従って英語で説明しましょう。

(1)  ［原級を用いて］
_____
_____

(2)  ［比較級を用いて］
_____
_____
_____

Makoto(10) Toru(18)

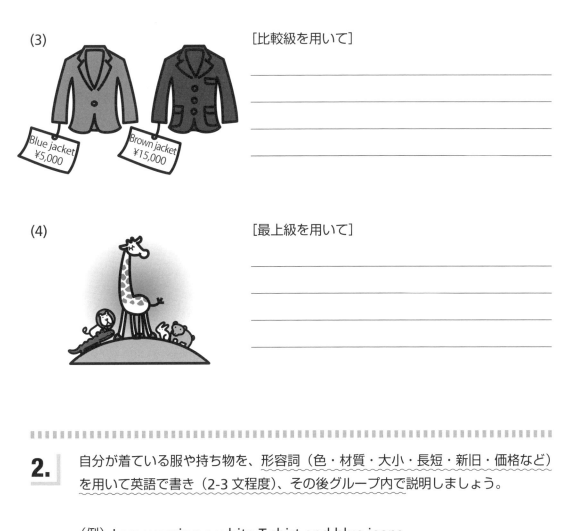

(3) [比較級を用いて]

(4) [最上級を用いて]

2. 自分が着ている服や持ち物を、形容詞（色・材質・大小・長短・新旧・価格など）を用いて英語で書き（2-3文程度）、その後グループ内で説明しましょう。

（例）I am wearing a white T-shirt and blue jeans.

📁 Assignment （グループワーク）

1. Warm-up で挙げた3つの商品について、値段をつけた上で具体的に英語で説明しましょう（各商品2文以上）。それから、グループで互いの商品を英語で比較しましょう。

（例）This is a white mug cup made in Japan. The price is 200 yen.

1) _____

2) _____

3) _____

2. 上に書いた商品を元に実際に仮想フリーマーケットを行いましょう。会話文の言い回しを使いましょう。値引き交渉も忘れずに！

👀 Let's Review! （形容詞・比較表現のまとめ）

- **形容詞**　1) 名詞を修飾する。This is an <u>old book</u>.

　　　　　　　＊ old は直後の名詞 book を修飾している。

　　　　　　2) 文の補語になる。<u>This book is old</u>.

- **比較表現**　1) 原級比較：A is as 形容詞 as B (is). Tom is as old as Judy.

　　　　　　　2) 比較級：A is 比較級 [-er] than B (is). Mike is taller than Sam.
　　　　　　　　ただし長いつづりの場合は more 形容詞 than ～ となる。
　　　　　　　　This picture is more beautiful than that one.

　　　　　　　3) 最上級：A is the 最上級 [-est] { in + [場所] / of + [all / the 数字] }

ただし長いつづりの場合は the most 形容詞 (in[of] ~) となる。
　　　　　　　　Helen is the most interesting girl in my class.

✓ Vocabulary　下の単語の意味が確認できたら、チェックを入れましょう。

☐ antique　　☐ cool　　☐ cotton　　☐ expensive　　☐ goods
☐ light　　☐ price　　☐ recommend

Unit 12 レポートの提出

よいレポートを書くためには、本を読むことが大事ですね。あなたはそれらの本をどうやって手に入れますか。

Warm-up （ペアワーク）

1. あなたは期末レポートを書くことになりました。必要な本のタイトルを自由に考えてリストを作りましょう。

Books which I need to read

Title	
Ex. "Omotenashi"	A book which I found on the Internet.
1. _____	A book which I borrowed from the library.
2. _____	A book which I bought at a book store.
3. _____	A book which my teacher recommended.

2. 1. のリストを基に、ペアになってお互いに何のレポートを書くのかを話し合いましょう。

Reading

Bob と Hana の会話を読んで以下の問いに答えましょう。

The deadline is tomorrow.

Bob: What are you reading, Hana?
Hana: The book which Professor Smith recommended in his ethics class. I have to read it by tomorrow to write a paper.
Bob: What is the book about?
Hana: It is a story about a girl whose life is suddenly changed. One day, she meets a person who looks just like her. After that, she has many unbelievable experiences.
Bob: What is the theme of the paper?
Hana: "How can your mind overcome unbelievable difficulties?"
Bob: I see. When you've submitted it, let's have lunch together.
Hana: Good idea! Where?
Bob: At an Italian restaurant which my cousin has recently opened.

Notes　deadline ▶ 締切　　ethics ▶ 倫理学　　paper ▶ レポート
　　　　　unbelievable ▶ 信じられない　overcome ▶ 克服する　submit ▶ 提出する

1. 上の会話文の中から関係代名詞を選び、それが説明している語と内容を抜き出しましょう。

説明されている語	関係代名詞	内容
		Professor Smith recommended in his ethics class
	whose	
		looks just like her
	which	

2. Hana が読んでいる本はどのような内容でしょうか。会話文を参考にして、日本語で説明しましょう。

3. Bob と Hana は、明日どこで昼食を取るつもりですか。次のイラストから選びましょう。

a

b

c

関係代名詞

関係代名詞を使って、「先行詞」と呼ばれる名詞を修飾することができます。

関係代名詞には、その役割に応じて、主格、目的格、所有格の3つがあります。

●**主　格**：関係代名詞の後に、「動詞」が続く。

　　先行詞が人　　→ Hana is a woman who has a brother. ハナは、弟がいる女性です。

　　先行詞が人以外 → This is a cartoon which was drawn by her.
　　　　　　　　　　これは、彼女によって描かれた漫画です。

●**目的格**：関係代名詞のあとに、「主語＋動詞」が続く。

　　先行詞が人　　→ Hana is a woman whom everyone knows.
　　　　　　　　　　ハナは、皆が知っている女性です。

　　先行詞が人以外 → This is a cartoon which everyone knows.
　　　　　　　　　　これは、皆が知っている漫画です。

●**所有格**：関係代名詞の後に、「名詞」が続く。

　　先行詞が人でも人以外でも → She has a brother whose name is Manabu.
　　　　　　　　　　　　　　　彼女にはマナブという名前の弟がいます。
　　　　　　　　　　　　　　　She lives in a house whose roof is red.
　　　　　　　　　　　　　　　彼女は赤い屋根の家に住んでいます。

 Listening （ペアワーク） 25

1.　音声を聴いて、（　）に適切な語を書き入れましょう。

(1) Who is the singer (　　　) you like best?

(2) Who is a person (　　　) words strongly influenced* you?　　*影響を与えた

(3) What is a TV program (　　　) you watched last night?

(4) What is the movie (　　　) impressed* you most?　　*感動させた

2. 1. の質問に、答えましょう。

(1) The singer whom I like best is _____.

(2) A person whose words strongly influenced me is _____.

(3) A TV program which I watched last night is _____.

(4) The movie which impressed me most is _____.

3. ペアになって、1.、2. の応答を練習しましょう。そして、表に友達の情報を書きましょう。表中の下線部には、友達の名前を書きましょう。

	答え
(1) The singer whom _____ likes best	
(2) A person whose words strongly influenced _____	
(3) A TV program which _____ watched last night	
(4) The movie which impressed _____ most	

Writing & Speaking （ペアワーク）

1. 2つの文を、関係代名詞を使って、1つにしましょう。また、できた文を訳しましょう。

（例）Hana is a woman. The woman loves cooking.
　　　2つの文で重複している the woman を関係代名詞 who に置き換える
　　　⇩
　　（答え）Hana is a woman who loves cooking.
　　　（ハナは料理が大好きな女性です。）

(1) I joined a party. The party was organized* by my classmate.　　*企画された
　→ _____
　訳) _____

(2) I met an American. He spoke Japanese very fluently*.　　*流ちょうに
　→ _____
　訳) _____

(3) Mari wore a pearl necklace. Her mother bought her the pearl necklace for her birthday.

→

訳) _____

(4) Take a look at a website. The website shows you nice restaurants in Osaka.

→

訳) _____

2.

(1) 関係代名詞を使って、下のイラストについて、できるだけ詳しく説明しましょう。

a

（例）Mt. Fuji is the mountain which every Japanese knows best.

b

（例）Kinkaku-ji is a temple which was built in 1397.

c

（例）Ryoma Sakamoto is a person whose name is well known in Japan.

(2) ペアになって、a〜cで作った英文を比べましょう。そして、友達が作った文も、それぞれ書き加えましょう。

📁 Assignment （ペアワーク）

あなたは、あるパーティーに参加しました。そこで、プロフィールカードに記入することになりました。下の表に、情報を英語で記入しましょう。次回の授業で、友達と情報を交換しましょう。

My name is _____

The food which I eat most: _____
The word which I like best: _____
A person who gives me energy: _____
The person whom I respect* most: _____

＊尊敬する

👀 Let's Review!　（関係代名詞のまとめ）

２つの文をつなぐ接続詞の働きと、代名詞の働きを兼ねる語。

- ●主　格：I have a sister who lives in New York.
  私には、ニューヨークに住む姉がいます。

  This is a novel which was written by him.
  これは、彼によって書かれた小説です。

- ●目的格：She is an actress whom everybody knows.
  彼女は、誰もが知っている女優です。

  This is a watch which my sister gave me.　これは、姉がくれた時計です。

- ●所有格：I have a friend whose father is a famous actor.
  私には、父親が有名な俳優である友達がいます。

  He has a dog whose name is Pochi.
  彼は、名前がポチという犬を飼っています。

✅ Vocabulary　下の単語の意味が確認できたら、チェックを入れましょう。

- ☐ cousin
- ☐ difficulty
- ☐ experience
- ☐ mind
- ☐ submit
- ☐ suddenly
- ☐ theme

Unit 13 どこに住んでいるの？

住む場所は、キャンパスライフの楽しさを左右する大切な要素です。あなたはどこに住んでいますか。

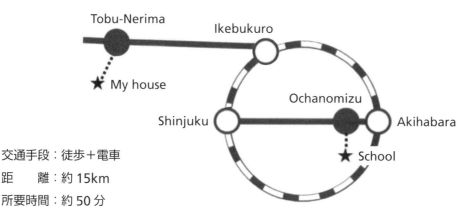

交通手段：徒歩＋電車
距　　離：約 15km
所要時間：約 50 分

Warm-up

あなたが住んでいる場所から学校までの略図を、上の図を参考にして、描きましょう。そして、交通手段、距離、所要時間について当てはまるものを下の□にチェックしましょう。

☐ by bus　　☐ by train　　☐ by bicycle　　☐ on foot　　☐ other _____

☐ 0-5 km　　☐ 6-20 km　　☐ 21-50 km　　☐ more than 50 km

☐ 0-10 min　☐ 11-30 min　☐ 31-60 min　　☐ more than 60 min

Reading

次の英文を読んで、後の問いに答えましょう。

Are you looking for a new apartment? (1) It is not easy to choose the right apartment. You should consider many factors such as cost, size, room layout, location, and rules.

Perhaps one of the most important factors is the location. (2) How far is it from campus? (3) How long does it take to campus? (4) It is very important to ask yourself these questions. You should choose an apartment close to your school. However, some schools are not in the city but in the country. They may be in an inconvenient location. If you live in an apartment in the country, there may not be any supermarkets, book stores, or grocery stores nearby. So if you want to choose the right apartment, you should also think about factors that make your daily life convenient.

Notes consider ▶ 考慮する   close to ▶ 〜に近い
inconvenient ▶ 不便な

1. アパート探しでは何を考慮すべきでしょうか。上の英文で述べられている要素7つを○で囲みましょう。

| 家賃 | 広さ | 間取り | セキュリティー | 防音 |
| 学校までの距離 | 通学時間 | 買い物の便利さ | 規則 |

2. (1) 〜 (4) の英文ではそれぞれ it を使って何を表しているのか、下から選んで（　）に書き入れましょう。

(1) (　　　　)
(2) (　　　　)
(3) (　　　　)
(4) (　　　　)

| 距離　時間　天候 |
| 暑さ寒さ　　to 以下の内容 |

「それは」と訳さない It

天候・暑さ寒さ・距離・時間などを表す場合や、仮の主語として、It が使われます。

It is sunny and warm today.

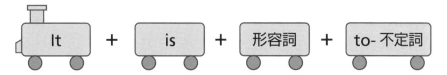

(a) To study English is important.

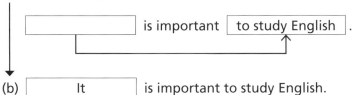

(b) [It] is important to study English.

(a) と (b) は同じ意味ですが、(b) は、(a) の長い主語を後ろに回して、そのあとの空白の部分に形式的な仮の主語 It を入れたものです。

Listening

マナブのブログについての音声を聴いて、(　) に適切な語を書き入れましょう。

CD 27

7:20 p.m., Apr. 6

(1) It's (^{1}　　) and really (^{2}　　) in winter here, so I'm very happy when spring comes around. All the classes at university started today. It is very (^{3}　　) to learn new things!

8:00 a.m., June 15

(2) It's (^{4}　　) o'clock in the morning. It's (^{5}　　) and (^{6}　　) now. It's a little (^{7}　　) to go to school in the rainy season.

9:05 p.m., Sep. 26

(3) I went to school to take an exam today. On my way home, it was raining heavily and I got soaking wet. It's (^{8}) and (^{9}) now because a typhoon is approaching.

8:45 p.m., Dec. 21

(4) I moved into a new apartment yesterday. It is only (^{10}) meters from here to my school. It takes about (^{11}) minutes to walk there.

Speaking （ペアワーク）

ペアになり、下の会話文を読む練習をしましょう。そして □ 内を下の絵の新しい情報と入れ替えて、ロールプレイをしましょう。

A: How far is it from your house to the station ?
B: It's about one kilometer .
A: How long does it take?
B: It takes ten minutes   on foot .

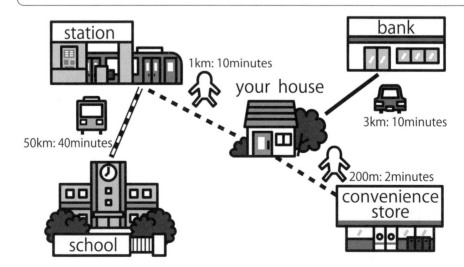

Writing （ペアワーク）

1. 次の英文を It を使って書き直しましょう。

（例）To say everything in English is difficult.
→ It is difficult to say everything in English.

(1) To run 100 meters in 10 seconds is very difficult.

→ _____

(2) To graduate from this school is not easy.

→ _____

(3) To choose good friends is important.

→ _____

(4) To exercise hard every day is not necessary.

→ _____

2. 上と下のイラストを自由に組み合わせて It を主語にした英文を作り、パートナーと意見交換しましょう。

(1)	(2)	(3)	(4)
pleasant	important	easy	difficult
study hard	sing English songs	swim in the sea	lose weight

(1) _____

(2) _____

(3) _____

(4) _____

📁 Assignment

あなたが住んでいる街をブログで紹介します。次の表現を使って、英文で書きましょう。

・It is（今日の天候や暑さ寒さ）.
・I live in（住んでいる場所）.
・It is（周辺の建物までの距離）. や It takes（所要時間）.
・It is (pleasant / exciting / important / easy / difficult) to *do*.

_____
_____
_____
_____

📖 Let's Review!　（「それは」と訳さない It）

●距離、時間、天候、暑さ寒さなどを表す It

[距離] It is two kilometers from here to the nearest station.
　　　ここから最寄り駅まで2キロある。

[時間] It takes 30 minutes on foot.
　　　歩いて30分かかる。

[天候・暑さ寒さ] It is hot and humid in summer here.
　　　ここの夏は蒸し暑い。

●後ろの長い主語を受ける形式主語の It

It is important to study a foreign language.
外国語を勉強することは大切だ。

✓ Vocabulary　下の語句の意味が確認できたら、チェックを入れましょう。

| ☐ by train | ☐ hot and humid | ☐ How far ...? | ☐ How long ...? |
| ☐ on foot | ☐ pleasant | ☐ snowy | ☐ windy |

宝くじが当たったらなあ

もし宝くじが当たったら、あなたならどうしますか。車を買うのになあ、海外旅行に行くのになあ・・・空想してみてください。

Warm-up

1. 例にならって、日本語で自分のことについて書きましょう。

〈単なる条件〉
（例）もしこのバッグを貸してくれたら、ランチをおごるよ。
・

〈現在の事実〉	〈過去の事実〉
（例）僕にはカノジョがいない。	（例）私はテスト勉強しなかった。
・	・

〈現在の願望〉 （現在の事実に反すること）	〈過去を振り返っての願望〉 （過去の事実に反する願望）
（例）カノジョがいればなあ。	（例）テスト勉強しておけばよかったなあ。
・	・

（例）もしカノジョがいれば、デートできるのになあ。	（例）もしテスト勉強していたら、いい点が取れたのになあ。
・	・

2. 記入した事柄をクラスメイトと見比べましょう。

2人の男子学生の会話を読んで、あとの問いに答えましょう。

Kazu : Hi, Taka. What's up?
Taka : I'm so bored. I have nothing to do.
Kazu : Oh, then why don't we go to USJ tomorrow?
Taka : I wish I could, but I can't. I have my part-time job.
Kazu : That's too bad. Then, how about this weekend?
Taka : Sunday would be okay. Wait a minute, just you and me?
　　　Two college boys going to USJ together?
Kazu : What do you mean?
Taka : We need to have girls with us.
Kazu : You're right, but actually we don't have girlfriends.
Taka : If we had girlfriends, we could ask them to join us. By the way,
　　　do you remember Maria?
Kazu : Of course. You liked her.
Taka : If I had been braver, I would have asked her out . But it's too late.
　　　She moved to Canada.
Kazu : Yeah. I'm sorry. Anyway, let's forget about girls. We can have fun
　　　without girls because USJ is full of exciting attractions.
Taka : True.

Notes　bored ▶ 退屈した　　brave ▶ 勇気のある
　　　　　ask ～ out ▶ ～をデートに誘う

1. 事実に反する願望や後悔を表現している文を抜き出し、日本語にしましょう。
（P.81 の仮定法参照）

(1) もし今～なら・・・のになあ（現在の事実に反すること）
（英）・
（日）・
（英）・
（日）・
(2) もしあの時～していたら・・・だったのになあ（過去の事実に反すること）
（英）・
（日）・

2. KazuとTakaに分かれて、ペアでロールプレイをしましょう。

仮 定 法

単に「条件」を表す「If（もし・・・）」ではなく、「事実とは異なること」を仮定するのが仮定法です。

●仮定法過去（現在の事実に反する仮定）→過去形を使う

If + 主語 + 過去形 , 主語 + would/could/might + 動詞原形
　もし今〜なら　　　　　　　　　　　　　　　…なのになあ

I wish + 主語 + 過去形
　今〜だったらいいのになあ

＊be動詞の過去形は"were"を使う

●仮定法過去完了（過去の事実に反する仮定）→過去完了形を使う

If + 主語 + had + 過去分詞 , 主語 + would/could/might + have + 過去分詞
　もしあの時〜だったら　　　　　　　　　　　…だったのになあ

I wish + 主語 + had + 過去分詞
　あの時〜だったらよかったのになあ

●その他「まるで〜のように」 as if 〜
　　　　「もし〜がなかったら…」Without 〜 , … / But for 〜 , …

Listening & Speaking 29

1. 音声を聴いて、（　）に単語を書き入れましょう。また、出来上がった英文を声に出して読みましょう。

(1) I wish I (　　　) (　　　) the lottery.
宝くじが当たったらなあ。

(2) I wish I (　　　) (　　　) harder.
もっと一生懸命勉強しておけばよかったなあ。

(3) What (　　　) you (　　　) if you (　　　) me?
もし君が僕だったらどうする。

(4) My father talks as if he (　　　) everything.
父は自分が何でも知っているかのように話す。

(5) "Can you help me?" "I wish I (　　　)."
「手伝ってくれない？」「ちょっと無理かな。」

(6) If I (　　　) the chance, I (　　　) (　　　) (　　　) live in the US.
もし機会があるなら、アメリカに住みたい。

2. 左の英文に続く文を右から選び線でつなぎましょう。次に音声を聴いて答えを確認し、声に出して読みましょう。　30

(1) But for your help,　　　・　　　・ as if I were a baby.

(2) Without air,　　　・　　　・ I couldn't have finished my report.

(3) My grandmother treats me ・　　　・ I would have run a marathon.

(4) If I hadn't gotten the flu, ・　　　・ we couldn't live on the earth.

Writing & Speaking （ペアワーク）

1. もし10億円が当たったら、あなたならどうしますか。例にならって絵を描いて、その絵が表す英文を書きましょう。

（例）
If I had one billion yen,
I would buy a big house.

If I had one billion yen…

2. クラスメイトに次の質問をして、答えを書き取りましょう。

Q. What would you do if you had one billion yen?

Partner's Name	Answer
（例）Keiko	She would buy a big house if she had one billion yen.
1.	
2.	
3.	

📁 Assignment

Warm-up で挙げた「現在の願望」「過去を振り返っての願望」「単なる条件」を、例にならって英文にしましょう。

(例) (1) I wish I had a girlfriend.
　　 (2) If I had a girlfriend, I could date her.
　　 (3) I wish I had studied harder for the test.
　　 (4) If I had studied harder for the test, I would have gotten a better score.
　　 (5) If you lend me this bag, I will treat you to lunch.

(1) _____
(2) _____
(3) _____
(4) _____
(5) _____

👀 Let's Review! （仮定法のまとめ）

●仮定法過去

　　If I knew her phone number, I would call her.

　　（今）もし彼女の電話番号を知っていれば、電話するのになあ。

　　I wish I knew her phone number.

　　（今）彼女の電話番号を知っていればなあ。

●仮定法過去完了

　　If I had known her phone number, I would have called her.

　　（あの時）もし彼女の電話番号を知っていたなら、電話したのになあ。

　　I wish I had known her phone number.

　　（あの時）彼女の電話番号を知っていたらなあ。

✅ Vocabulary　下の単語の意味が確認できたら、チェックを入れましょう。

☐ bored　　☐ brave　　☐ college　　☐ forget
☐ have fun　☐ move　　☐ part-time job　☐ remember

Unit 15 Review Test

学籍番号 _____ 氏名 _____

/ 60 点

Part 1 (Unit 1~7) / 30 点

1. 次の英語に合う日本語の意味を下の語群から選び、記号で答えなさい。

1. opposite (　)　　2. major (　)　　3. serve (　)　　4. science (　)

5. rarely (　)　　6. healthy (　)　　7. advice (　)　　8. discover (　)

9. quiet (　)　　10. add (　)　　11. furniture (　)　　12. bread (　)

13. lose weight (　)　　14. independence (　)　　15. on weekends (　)

a. 独立	b. 減量する	c. 週末に	d. 専攻科目	e. めったに〜ない
f. 反対側の	g. 静かな	h. 加える	i. 発見する	j. 健康的な
k. 科学	l. 家具	m. 料理を出す	n. 助言	o. パン

2. 次の文の（　）に入る適切な語句を選び、記号で答えなさい。

1. Let's (　).

　　a. dance　　　　b. danced　　　　c. dancing

2. "(　) do you work part-time?" — "Once a week."

　　a. What time　　b. How often　　c. How many

3. It (　) be sunny tomorrow.

　　a. will　　　　　b. is　　　　　　c. was

4. I have to ( ) now.

   a. leaving   b. left   c. leave

5. Akiko plays with ( ) dog every day.

   a. she   b. hers   c her

6. How ( ) sugar do you need to make cookies?

   a. many   b. much   c. weight

7. My sister usually gets up ( ) 10 o'clock on Sundays.

   a. on   b. in   c. at

8. I teach ( ) Japanese.

   a. he   b. him   c. his

9. ( ) he usually spend a lot of money on parties?

   a. Does   b. Is   c. Has

10. By ( ) books, we learn a lot of new things.

    a. read   b. reading   c. to read

11. Everyone calls him ( ).

    a. to Ken   b. for Ken   c. Ken

12. Please finish the report ( ) the end of this month.

    a. over   b. by   c. on

13. My parents want ( ) to the sea in summer.

    a. go   b. going   c. to go

14. Don't ( ) the water and the oil.

  a. to mix   b. mixing   c. mix

15. You don't ( ) to wear a tie.

  a. will   b. have   c. can

Part 2 (Unit 8 ~14) / 30 点

1. 次の英語に合う日本語の意味を下の語群から選び、記号で答えなさい。

1. huge ( )   2. antique ( )   3. recommend ( )

4. hot and humid ( )   5. cousin ( )   6. dish ( )

7. win a match ( )   8. prepaid ( )   9. on foot ( )

10. submit ( )   11. go skiing ( )   12. bored ( )

13. part-time job ( )   14. expect( )   15.brave ( )

a. 徒歩で	b. 退屈した	c. 巨大な	d. 期待する
e. 蒸し暑い	f. 試合に勝つ	g. 食器	h. 推薦する
i. アルバイト	j. いとこ	k. 提出する	l. 先払いの
m. スキーに行く	n. 骨董品	o. 勇気のある	

2. 次の文の（ ）に入る適切な語句を選び、記号で答えなさい。

1. Ken ( ) talking on the phone right now.

  a. is   b. are   c. am

2. Which is ( ), Tokyo or Osaka?

  a. big   b. bigger   c. the biggest

3. I wish I ( ) a girlfriend.

   a. has   b. had   c. having

4. I have never ( ) such an exciting game.

   a. see   b. saw   c. seen

5. She is one of the ( ) tennis players I have ever seen.

   a. best   b. better   c. good

6. The person ( ) beef steaks is my brother.

   a. is grilling   b. grilled   c. grilling

7. Finally, the thief was ( ) by the police.

   a. brought   b. caught   c. taught

8. If I had studied harder for the test, I ( ) a better score.

   a. would gotten   b. would have gotten   c. am gotten

9. My sister ( ) in London since 2010.

   a. has come   b. has gone   c. has been

10. I know a woman ( ) son is a famous singer.

   a. who   b. whose   c. whom

11. It ( ) fifteen minutes to walk to the station.

   a. is   b. has   c. takes

12. The yen-dollar rate is ( ) by the blue line.

   a. shown   b. shows   c. showing

13. He is a boy (　) everyone knows.

    a. whose　　　　b. which　　　　c. whom

14. (　) is nice and sunny today.

    a. He　　　　b. It　　　　c. There

15. If I (　) his phone number, I would call him.

    a. know　　　　b. knew　　　　c. known

人称代名詞一覧

人称	数		主格 〜は、が	所有格 〜の	目的格 〜を、に	所有代名詞 〜のもの	再帰代名詞 〜自身
一人称	単数		I	my	me	mine	myself
	複数		we	our	us	ours	ourselves
二人称	単数		you	your	you	yours	yourself
	複数						yourselves
三人称	単数	男性	he	his	him	his	himself
		女性	she	her	her	hers	herself
		中性	it	its	it	無し	itself
	複数		they	their	them	theirs	themselves

TEXT PRODUCTION STAFF

edited by　　　　　編集
Eiichi Kanno　　　菅野 英一
Masato Kogame　　小亀 正人

English-language editing by　　英文校閲
Bill Benfield　　　　　　　　ビル・ベンフィールド

cover design by　　表紙デザイン
Ruben Frosali　　ルーベン・フロサリ

illustrated by　　イラスト
IOK Co., Ltd.　　株式会社 イオック

CD PRODUCTION STAFF

recorded by　　　　　　　吹き込み者
Howard Colefield (AmE)　ハワード・コールフィールド（アメリカ英語）
Rachel Walzer (AmE)　　レイチェル・ワルザー（アメリカ英語）

English Locomotion
参加して学ぶ総合英語

2015年1月20日　初版発行
2024年3月5日　第9刷発行

編 著 者　幸重 美津子　仲川 浩世
著　　者　赤尾 美和　西垣 佐理　岡本 由紀子
　　　　　尾鍋 智子　大内 和正　千田 愛
英文校閲　Carl Nommensen

発 行 者　佐野 英一郎
発 行 所　株式会社 成美堂
　　　　　〒101-0052　東京都千代田区神田小川町3-22
　　　　　TEL 03-3291-2261　FAX 03-3293-5490
　　　　　https://www.seibido.co.jp

印刷・製本　　三美印刷(株)

ISBN 978-4-7919-3383-9　　　　　　　　　　　　　　Printed in Japan

・落丁・乱丁本はお取り替えします。
・本書の無断複写は、著作権上の例外を除き著作権侵害となります。